IN MY BACKYARD

robins

by Kate Riggs

CREATIVE EDUCATION
CREATIVE PAPERBACKS

Published by Creative Education and Creative Paperbacks
P.O. Box 227, Mankato, Minnesota 56002
Creative Education and Creative Paperbacks are imprints of
The Creative Company
www.thecreativecompany.us

Design and production by Chelsey Luther
Art direction by Rita Marshall
Printed in China

Photographs by Alamy (Gaertner, William Leaman), Corbis
(Gary Carter, Chris Knorr/Design Pics, Jouko van der
Kruijssen), Dreamstime (Hsagencia, Isselee, Tamara Kulikova,
Brian Kushner), Flickr (Eric Bégin, Chuck Roberts, Matt
Ward), iStockphoto (ChristiLaLiberte, stanley45), National
Geographic Creative (DAVID LIITTSCHWAGER, DARLYNE
A. MURAWSKI), Science Source (Steve & Dave Maslowski),
Shutterstock (Dionisvera, dragon_fang, David Spates)

Library of Congress Cataloging-in-Publication Data
Riggs, Kate.
Robins / by Kate Riggs.
p. cm. — (In my backyard)
Includes bibliographical references and index.
Summary: A high-interest introduction to the life cycle of
robins, including how fledglings develop, their varied diet,
threats from predators, and the treetop habitats of these
backyard animals.

ISBN 978-1-60818-701-0 (hardcover)
ISBN 978-1-62832-297-2 (pbk)
ISBN 978-1-56660-737-7 (eBook)
1. Robins—Juvenile literature.

QL696.P288 R54 2016
598.8/42—dc23   2015039246

CCSS: RI.1.1, 2, 3, 4, 5, 6, 7; RI.2.1, 2, 4, 5, 6, 7, 10; RF.1.1, 3, 4;
RF.2.3, 4

First Edition HC 9 8 7 6 5 4 3 2 1
First Edition PBK 9 8 7 6 5 4 3 2 1

Contents

You are walking down the street. Is someone whistling? Wings flap up above. A bird with an orange chest lands in front of you. It is a robin!

In the northern United States, seeing the first robin is a sign of springtime.

5

The first baby robins hatch in the spring. There are two to five eggs in a brood. Robin chicks do not have feathers. The chicks become fledglings as they grow feathers.

The chicks (right) do not open their eyes until about 5 days after hatching.

Robins leave the nest at two weeks old. Young robins cannot fly well yet. Watch them hop in the grass! They stay near their parents for another two weeks.

fledgling

Fledglings often still need their parents to feed them food while they learn to fly.

Adult robins live all over North America. They like the woods and grass-lands. They also like to be near people. In the winter, robins live in flocks.

Robins that live near people may make use of birdbaths in yards and parks.

11

Robins fly to wherever there is food. They eat insects, worms, fruits, and berries. Have you seen a robin with a worm? If it does not eat the worm, it will take it to its nest.

Besides berries and worms, robins sometimes catch very small fish to eat.

Robins work hard to get food for their babies. They may look for food all day! Late in the summer, adults molt. They get ready to fly somewhere else for the winter.

Robins have several broods a year and build a new nest for each one.

Squirrels, crows, and snakes try to take robin eggs and chicks. The parents guard the nest. They chase away predators! Other big birds hunt adult robins.

Robins make chirping and chucking sounds to warn of danger.

A robin carrying twigs and dead grass may be making a nest. Look for nests near your home. Listen for the robin's cheerful song!

Male robins sing to females and help gather sticks to make a nest.

Activity: Listening for Songs

Robins are known for their happy songs. Some people think a robin's song sounds like this: "cheerily, cheery-up, cheery-o, cheerily." The next time you hear birds singing, try to pick out the robin!

Materials you need: pencil or marker and paper; phone or tablet (optional)

What Do You Hear?

1. A lot of songbirds can be heard early in the morning or as the sun is going down. Listen for the sounds birds make where you live. Are they like whistles or flutes? Is it the same sound over and over? Does the voice sound high or low?

2. Write down what the songs sound like to you. If you have a phone or tablet, record the songs to keep listening to them!

3. Imagine what the birds might be saying. Are they calling to each other? Are they sad or angry? Maybe they are calm and happy.

Have a friend listen to the birds with you. What does he think the songs sound like?

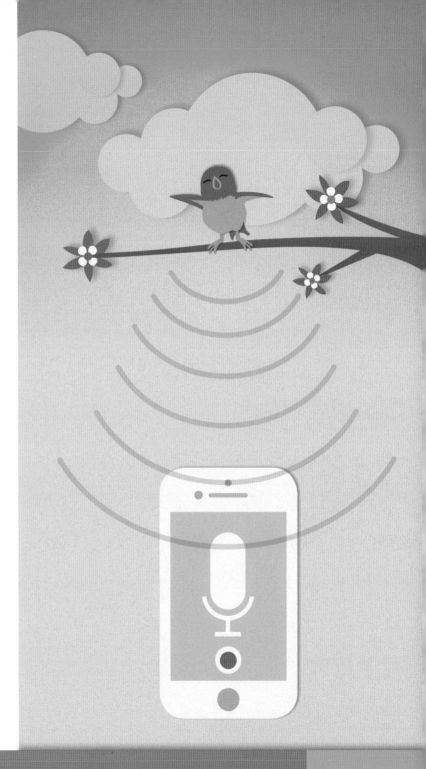

Glossary

brood: a group of animal babies born at the same time; robins have two to three broods a year

flocks: groups of birds that live together; robins flock together in the winter

hatch: to break out of an egg

molt: to shed or lose old feathers so that new ones can grow

predators: animals that hunt other animals for food

Read More

Schuetz, Kari. *Birds*.
Minneapolis: Bellwether Media, 2013.

Willis, Nancy Carol. *The Robins in Your Backyard*.
Middletown, Del.: Birdsong Books, 2000.

Websites

KidZone: American Robin
http://www.kidzone.ws/animals/birds/american-robin.htm
Review what you know about robins using worksheets and other activities.

National Wildlife Federation: Toasty Robins
http://www.nwf.org/kids/family-fun/recipes/toasty-robin-with-peanut-butter-and-jelly.aspx
Follow the directions to make a robin out of toast!

Note: Every effort has been made to ensure that the websites listed above are suitable for children, that they have educational value, and that they contain no inappropriate material. However, because of the nature of the Internet, it is impossible to guarantee that these sites will remain active indefinitely or that their contents will not be altered.

Index